My Cat Is Up To Something

Hal Purton

BookLeaf Publishing

Presentation by *BookLeaf Publishing*

Web: www.bookleafpub.com

E-mail: info@bookleafpub.com

ISBN: 9789357696869

First edition 2023

DEDICATION

For Bubbles, Kashmir, and all the other cats I haven't had the chance to snuggle yet.

ACKNOWLEDGEMENT

I'd like to thank the English Department at my old school, without whom I never would have understood the nuances and subtext behind 'The Very Hungry Caterpillar'.

PREFACE

This is collection of poems for when you're sitting down with your cat on your lap, and you really want to get up but you also really don't want to wake him - because you know that if the roles were reversed and you were curled up on someones lap and they moved, you'd be pretty annoyed yourself, wouldn't you?

So you just sort of sit there in this weird limbo state, not wanting to move, but also desperate not to stay in one place forever...

Listen

Today,
I will step outside of thought
Into a place I know too well,
And listen
To the beating call of silence.

The world was quiet here
(but now my headaches have no end)
And this beauty, now unbearable,
Has no comfort left to share.
Ruined with truth
And the tarnished meaning underneath
But perfected in the stillness.

So I drift
From a world where thought is king,
And listen
to a place unstained by reason
Where ignorance reigns quietly.

Tomorrow Men

The place where the tomorrow men live
Is full of tomorrow folk.
The tomorrow men live in tomorrow tree homes
Made from tomorrow oak.

The tomorrow women it seems
Have soft tomorrow skin.
It's often hard to see where they end
And the tomorrow earth begins.

But tomorrow folk live in a wonderful place
And I clearly don't belong.
If I can't control my tomorrow deeds
Will I right my tomorrow wrongs?

If I could see the yesterday folk
And look at yesterday men
I'd see that there's nothing at all stopping us
From belonging to that crowd again.

The yesterday men are rowdy,
Common, and plain, and rude.
I much prefer the tomorrow folk culture
And the tomorrow folk food.

But all the tomorrow men live far away
And the yesterday men are dead.
So renounce any worry, remorse or dismay
And live in the present instead.

a poem I wrote whilst very happy and very very drunk

All that's left is his smile
The summertide lips curled like the moon
A crescent life untwined by fate.

Meet me in the roses.
You smell of me:
Soft, warm, and
Kind of like the garden.

I am without.
But we are nothing together:
Emptiness, and art.

A Poem To Be Read Under The Covers On A Quiet Afternoon

This place is warm.
The sounds are quiet here.
You can hear the rustling bedsheets,
Drawn over us
Like a cave
And the rain casting blurred shadows
Beyond the window.

Our lazy eyes trace over words,
Hardly reading,
But listening, hushed,
To the sound the pages make,
With our heads together
And our muted bodies touching warmly.
Now, safe from any realness,
We respectfully ignore
That noisy world outside

This impenetrable stillness
Which sings to me now
A soft melody.
The kind that you could listen to for hours

And still feel as safe
And as loved
And as still
As when it first held you on that rainy afternoon.

If I had a soft place like that,
I would have known
That love is
Pointlessly written
But eerie and wonderful
And that its end is abrupt
And bitter
But lingers irresistibly,
Like a lazy song's final note,
Or the last line of a sad poem
That neither of us can remember.

A Poem About Falling Asleep With The Right Person In Your Arms

I know the world is messy.
Sometimes, in the night,
When it is very quiet
And the darkness spreads like a veil
To tint this tangled place,
In a fuzzy sort of clarity,
You can lie on the bed
And pretend
For a silent moment
That everything's alright,
And that it all
Somehow
Makes a little more sense.

And I hope
In nights like these,
When you need someone
To remind you not to think
I'll be there too
And we can lie there together,
Silent, and still
And blissfully hidden

From a world far too full
With words
And thoughts
And people
To care about sleepyheads like us.

(They can’t see us anyway)
We’re under the covers now.
Holding each other so close
And so tight
That finally
The world stops moving for a moment
And slows down for once
To a still calmness,
Where we are peaceful, and real,
Breathing warm comfort in each other’s ears.
And it is very quiet here, alone with you.
And everything makes a little more sense.
And it is very, very comfy.

A Poem About Nice Smells And Pretty Smiles And Other Lovely Things

Holly's train gets in at four.
I sit here, an hour or two before.
She'll turn up bright and overjoyed
And I will melt into her warm void.

But I must wait in isolation
And weary anticipation,
So I will store my woes upon a higher shelf
And think up some happiness myself.

Every image in my mind:
One lost, one old, one left behind
Will blossom in me like a lonely flower
In such a mean and melancholic hour.

And she is there, among them all,
And she is fair, and she is tall,
And the song that I can hear her sing
Is what connects all Lovely Things.

A quiet, soothing, saddish tune,
Which tints this warm, late afternoon

In hues unique but not unpleasant.
How sweet a sound to such a weary peasant!

She has that smile – soft and kind,
That makes your coiled heart unwind,
That makes you weak, teary-eyed,
Twisty, and wonderful inside.

Nervous, eager, meek and strong
Like rousing battlesong,
A smile for which all breathing men
Would die again, and again, and again.

A look that turns the strongest chest,
Lips that have no sins confess'd,
And eyes that lock you into place
Enraptured by that beaming face.

The smell of unpaved country lanes,
The forest after rain,
Will comfort those who stay too long
Paralysed by nature's evensong.

The skyline flirting with the tops of trees,
The gentle buzzing of the bees
And flowers blushing in the fields and glades,
And lovers loving in the shade.

This art seems ever hidden from us all,

And questions always seem to fall
On ears that to not hear or care
Who, or what, or when, or where.

So, when you think of Lovely Things,
Don't let some moron's rude aroma
Pierce your musings with a nasty glare.
I like getting lost in thought;
No one interrupts me there.

Lola Said She Liked Me

The Earth is dull and rotten,
And Time is going mad.
But Lola said she liked me,
So perhaps things aren't so bad.

My world was full of weeping,
A wailing litany.
But Lola said she liked me
And soothed my agony.

Old feelings tried to catch me.
They chased me miles and miles.
But Lola said she liked me,
And now my heart is smiles.

You may insult me, call it Weakness,
Try to put me in my place
But I will stand there, arms folded,
A cocky grin across my face.

And I will boast it to the heavens
(Or whatever rules above),
For what is Time, the World, or Death
Compared to honest love?

In the light and in the darkness,
In Paradise or Hell,
Though all fortunes turn against me,
Lola likes me. I am well.

My Cat Is Up To Something

my cat is up to something.
he leaves each night
to do his secret work

and comes back at first light
with such a self-satisfied air
that is makes me wonder
what, if anything, he does out there?

does he hunt, or guard his borders?
terrorise the neighbourhood?
what is that scrappy bastard doing?
lord knows it can't be good.

perhaps it is nothing,
but those moments, in the mornings
where we lock eyes, cat and brother,
and stare wordlessly at each other...

his chilly smell, bush and grass me,
fresh from my early bath
two scents, two scoundrels
wearing masks...

it makes me feel as though he is daring me to
ask -
simply so that he can say
(in his own smug and silent way)
“i’m not telling you. go away.”

so, I shall simply not enquire.
i will, instead, greet him with the smile of a
fellow liar.
though we both know what is left unsaid,
neither of us will say it,

because we are silly, prideful little creatures
who made up this stupid game, and play it,
acting out this façade of spite
until he leaves again tonight.

and,

though admitting it may make me sick,
i am very fond of this furry little prick.

Wave Goodbye

I can’t go inside just yet.
I haven’t said ‘I love you’ to the Ocean,

And I’m wet.

Be Silly!

I used to lie, crying in bed,
Trying to think two thoughts ahead.
Juggling like an anxious clown
My tears, my fears, my snivelling crown.

But here I feel quite at home,
Like Romulus within his Rome.
Conforming to a world insane
Does wonders for the Jester's brain.

I urge you, be you as you are:
Give up your sanity, wounds and scars.
Do not accept this mediocre sadness;
There is always a home for you in madness.

It is a lovely safety harness,
Bathing in this true bizarreness.
To be human is to be malicious,
Those who oppose are far too vicious.

Temptation, lust and riddles,
Beginnings, end and middles,
And devils playing fiddles
In the woods at night.

It is noble, this persisting,
This dedication to resisting.
But something about it isn't quite enticing
Like a cupcake topped with too much icing.

There is no shame in letting go,
In giving up, or saying no,
In going mad, or blending in.
Far too many call it sin.

But the devil's home can be yours too.
Hell would never deny you
Access to a warm embrace.
Welcoming smiles fill this place.

Be not forlorn, be not afraid.
This sadness, it will surely fade.
But sanity is for the living,
Pity them, and be forgiving.

They must struggle on the earth
For illusions called "purpose" and "worth".
The only thing we should desire
Is love, and cake, and wildfire.

We look too often to the past,
To things we know can never last.
To wanting, seeking every pleasure.
We cannot have both life and leisure.

There are worms in the sky, and birds
underground.
Because everything is the wrong way round.
We are fed by the hungry, and led by the blind.
Red are the hands of all humankind.

In darkness, death and burning,
And everlasting yearning
For a world that won't stop turning
There are feelings quite concerning.

An itch, a nag, residual
In every individual,
A maddening dream for us each,
Elusive, two thoughts out of reach.

But madness has this dream unfurled:
We are far too serious in this world.
Emotion is our rotten ocean,
A beauty, ruined by devotion.

Full of frowning, sneering, glaring,
And of crying, jeering, staring,
Dancing, doing, dying, daring.
Without this poison you call "caring"

You can live, free of all this strife,
Living a wonderfully bonkers life!

Be you sad, or sick, or chilly:

Smile! Laugh!
Be silly!

The Puzzle Man

The Puzzle Man wears an invisible gown.
His heart, perplexed but beating.
All his words are upside-down,
He cannot stop repeating:

"I am a riddle, hatching a plot,
Solved by the puzzle that time forgot."

Ringing the final, earsplitting bell,
Singing his song, whose hymn,
Is a secret you must never tell
Because it would only confuse him.

"I am a riddle, hatching a plot,
Solved by the puzzle that time forgot."

He loves all the old puzzle games,
And he's been more than once 'round the joint.
And he's quite invested, and far too ashamed
To ever stop at this point.

"I am a riddle, hatching a plot,
Solved by the puzzle that time forgot."

He watches with ink smeared over his eyes

And listens with wool in his ears,
Because he knows he never understands
Anything he sees or hears.

"I am a riddle, hatching a plot,
Solved by the puzzle that time forgot."

He rides around in wheelbarrows,
Eats lemons for his scurvy.
All his friends are straight as arrows;
He is topsy-turvy.

"I am a riddle, hatching a plot,
Solved by the puzzle that time forgot.
Nothing here to stare at,
Everything to see.
For I am the man standing there in the mirror,
And all these faces look the same to me."

We Are Sick of These Goodbyes

"Would it be alright, my dear
If, only to dry my tears,
I stopped for just a moment here?"

There are far too many endings
To fall apart over just one more
With one fewer would we grin and cheer?
Our cosy future isn't clear.
But now, far less than before,
Those wailing monsters that I saw
In horrid visions reappear.

And there I will find,
In the corners of my mind,
Her, hiding in plain sight,
Disguised as love in kind.

But oh, she cries, she cries.
We are sick of these goodbyes.

I will walk away from her, and sigh,
Cursing myself for saying goodbye.
Though she is gone, some part might linger too
In me,

In myself and what I do,
As though a viper, hidden in the hay
That knows no heartbreak, or dismay
Could watch, and tentatively say:

"I have seen them weep, and cry.
I have seen them say goodbye.
Why must they tear themselves away?
Why? Oh, heavens, why?"

I do not know!
But she is a serpent of my own,
That has found her way into my brain,
Slithering like a coiled chain,
Pulled by scholars, to explain
Why every breath becomes a groan.
Why I walk alone,
In shame,
Like that first of sinners, Cain.

She is ever-present,
The voice inside my head,
As close as when she laid with me in bed.
Whispering, inches apart,
Though seen from far away,
And growing more lovely,
More lovely every day.
That, my sadness would betray.

And oh, I cry, I cry.
We are sick of these goodbyes.

I have seen her at her best.
And I have seen all the rest.
She is with me, in all forms and places.
She is with me while I tie my laces.
To say one word would be to accept
That ceaseless chain
That she has kept,
Rusted from goodbyes that we have wept.

She is comfort, home,
My dreams, and my delight.
She is my darling parasite.

i wrote this while i was high and also extremely hungry

Everything is the right volume.
My background screening into silence.
I feel like half a headache,
Melting into everything I touch,
Tracing them internally.

My feet feel like mine,
But not what I was born with,
As though a clumsy devil
Is guiding me away.

And everything is
softly sluggish,
A lazy kind of thickness.

And everything
Is the right

Volume.

Ode to a Sausage Roll

The ground is hard under my feet,
The taste of toothpaste hanging on my tongue
I ignore my burning lungs
And the blisters underneath
Panting through the sausage roll
Clenched between my minty teeth.
I haven't done the reading,
But in fairness, it was really long.
Even if I'm losing time,
Im listening to a good song, and my stomach
isn't rumbly.
And in any case,
I'd rather be late than hungry.

A chant comes to me as I climb the steps
And stumble to a seat, the roll's wrapper stuffed
into my tote.
Murmuring it under my breath
As I furiously scribble notes.
By the time the hour's voice has drawled,
I pause, and look at what I've scrawled:

'Salt in my mouth,
Beer in my gut.
My eyes wide open,

My ears half shut.
Why must everything unhealthy
Be so delicious, and so cheap?
Oh, how unstoppable I'd be
With ten seconds' extra sleep.'

I wish I could pretend this is how I feel.
But life's a treat,
And that treat is tasty,
(and I'm pretty sure it's real).
I am with some wonderfully fun people
In a marvellous place,
Wrapped in my warm pastry rhyme.
And we are all having a lovely time.

Dark Mirrors

Impressionism:
When the vision glazes over,
And dares itself into true Seeing,
And the shapes and colours of the not yet faded
Earth
Blend together,
Blurring the lines of meaning and of sight,
Swirling from impermanence to life.

And we weep,
Us fools who care to see.
For we must,
As our duty to the Rain and to the Moon
And the reflections of our wringing hands
In dark mirrors we call Eyes.
Which show us for once,
Not how the world looks,
But how it is, quivering,

Curled up
In the corner of its horrid beauty,
Exposed in lust and reverence:
Naked, wailing,
Full of tears.

Blank Canvas

Sing me that song again.
The simple tune that we hummed together
Before those recollections festered,
When we were too tired think anymore.

Wrench me free of this white prison,
This petrifying vault,
As empty as the heavens
And as senseless as any might imagine.

There is nothing more terrifying
Than the thought of starting over,
Of going through it all again.
I am grateful that we only live once.

But were I to be torn away,
At the moment of escape, of triumph,
To be thrust back into that world,
Would I know? Would I care?
Would I remember that this had been
My most dreadful nightmare?

And I think, perhaps,
That the most frightening part
Is that, under these assumptions,

It has probably already happened.

And that longing for ignorance,
For a way back, for a way to forget
Is ripping me in half,
Splitting me from my uncertainty to my
obsession.

These dwellings are far too loud,
And my envy for those whose heads are soft,
And quiet, and serene,
Enrages me beyond all thought.

They can sing, and write, and speak,
Unbothered, because they do not create for
purpose.
Their purpose is something intangible,
inexpressible,
They are born to live; not to stay alive.

It is all I can do, at night, in the dark,
To pound my brain into submission,
To focus, vehemently, on those irresistible
distractions,
That shield me from the one thought that has
always,
Since its first conception,
Wrought inescapable despair:

"Go back. Start again."

It is a shard of ice within my heart.
There is far less finality in birdsong.

Thursday

It's not quite the evening yet.
There is some kind of lingering hardness in the
air,
Like the end of a dim headache.
Five, then six o'clock rolls by,
And with it, a sky that seems indifferent to the
day
Has blackened over, rolling into dusk.
This in-between time
Is wrapping me in calm confusion.
The world in this moment feels out of rhythm,
Though still beating to its own time,
A comforting consistency.

And this lack of certainty is all too appealing
As the week nears its end.
As though everyone has had enough of worrying
And is about to quietly give up.
But something is urging them
To hold on
In a small way.
Not completely, but just enough,
Just the right amount
To stop taking everything so seriously
And live, contented

In this drowsy in-between time
Where familiar smiles carry us to bed.

She is lying on me, fast asleep.
Her eyes are closed, and she is soft.
There is something very Thursday about her.

A Poem About A Lover Running Their Fingers Through Your Hair

One day, not long ago,
I fell asleep.

(I remember it well)

I was lying on my front, with my arms folded underneath me,
Supporting my chin.

(I remember it very well)

Her hands were in my hair.
And in my head, where there should be thoughts,
There was nothing but a pleasant hum,
A gentle, soothing buzz.

(I remember it extremely well. It was incredibly relaxing)

Her absent-minded scratchings
Were a rake to my leaf-strewn mind.

Collecting my worry into a mound, a pile.
I will jump into it later, and scatter them again,
But for now, they are out of thought.

(I am beginning to remember less well)

And the line between awareness and silence,
Between existence and oblivion
Began to shiver.
Not in a frightened way,
But in the way that someone's lips
Might cheerfully tremble
When they are holding back a cheeky smile.

(I am remembering only vague aspects now, but I do not mind)

And that is where I crossed over.
Set myself down to rest,
While she blurred me out of consciousness.
In a delicious way,
She smudged me gently into sleep.

(I do not remember anything after this - I was, as I understand, snoozing happily beside her, quite content)

Read This In A Deep And Foreboding Voice

It is foul. It is vile.
It stinks of scum, of bile.
It is sickening, like mould,
And random, uncontrolled.
Toss a body on the pile
So the fire won't grow cold,
And watch them, all the while
Like a vengeful crocodile.

They are smirking in denial,
As though attempting to beguile,
But this hatred, now so old
Is not so easily exiled.
The bloodcurdling toll
As dreadfully foretold,
With that coward's grimy smile
Has climbed a thousandfold.

But that smell that I adore,
That enduring petrichor
The salt, the sand, the breeze,
The sunlight on the seas.
All grim and ghastly thoughts
Are sunk and drowned by these

Like so many dreams before.
So many vanquished, now no more.

Anxious, nervous, tense.
Their venom: violence.
Shielded by something fake,
Some adamant pretence
Delivered by a snake.
Whose fangs might tear, and quake
That delicate defence,
Their fashioned, fractured firmaments.

The word is 'quiver'.
Emerging from the river,
Cold things must hide the meek,
Bite back that icy shiver
And flee, with flame, the wretched creek
Numb, yet championed by the weak
Whose trust is in the tortured giver,
Like that Titan, and his liver.

Ten Thousand Hedgehogs

I lost my way in the woods, and cried.
But before my silent tears had dried,
A most unusual figure came to me
And sized me up, quite curiously.

I sniffed, and rose, and wiped my eyes.
This creature was less than half my size,
Yet walked with such authority
That I felt far smaller than he.

I peered at this creature that I faced,
And trembling, stepped where he had paced,
Mimicking his frenzied haste
As though I might be giving chase.

And suddenly, I was not alone,
I sat upon a woody throne.
I was still, from the roots up to the tree.
Ten thousand hedgehogs followed me.

And many of them danced, and played,
In a manner I could not dissuade,
And so I joined them, truly hooked.
What an ass I must have looked.

And all of us acknowledged
That otherworldly college
Of poets, artists, kings,
And other glorious things

That lawyers, bankers, priests,
And other nasty beasts
Could never supersede.
All lost, all lost indeed.

They would not descend so low
As to frolic to and fro
With the squirrels, and the frogs,
And ten thousand hedgehogs.

They see not, from their observatory
The joys of true absurdity.
The free man screams, runs wild, and then
relaxes,
So make art within this canvas, child,
And never pay your taxes.

A Poem To End A Lazy Day With

There are many, many things
I wish I could still do,
But there will be time to do them tomorrow.

It is no use pretending that I could have done them today.
There was not enough time,
Not enough driving me.

And it is unhelpful, worrying over such things,
Because I know, in the end,
They will matter less than I could have possibly foreseen.

They will get done, tomorrow or another day.
At this moment, they do not exist.
These problems are for the future us to solve.

Get distracted by something else now.
You have earned that.
Interrupt yourself, and find something lovely in the real world.

For now, I will allow myself to rest

In the knowledge that I've done my best.

And -

Excuse me,
But my cat has just done
A very big yawn

And I need to go congratulate him.

www.ingramcontent.com/pod-product-compliance
Lightning Source LLC
Chambersburg PA
CBHW062203160726
48282CB00027B/970
9789357696869